'The Shepherdess of the Alps'. English, 1790-1800. Silk and wool on silk, with painted faces. From a play in verse by J. F. Marmontel published in Paris in 1767. The scene shows Adelaide hearing Fortrose, disguised as a shepherd, playing his hautboy. From an engraving by Angelica Kauffman published in London in 1785. A similar embroidery in mirror image belongs to the Society for New England Antiquities and is labelled 'Attention, wrought by Ruth Alley' (of Salem). (The Lady Lever Art Gallery.)

EMBROIDERED GEORGIAN PICTURES

Margaret Swain

Shire Publications Ltd

CONTENTS

Published in 1994 by Shire Publications Ltd, Cromwell House, Church Street, Princes Risborough, Buckinghamshire HP27 9AA, UK. Copyright © 1994 by Margaret Swain. First edition 1994. Shire Album 307. ISBN 0 7478 0256 4.

Printed in Great Britain by CIT Printing Services, Press Buildings, Merlins Bridge, Haverfordwest, Dyfed SA61 1XF.

British Library Cataloguing in Publication Data: Swain, Margaret. Embroidered Georgian Pictures. – (Shire Albums; No. 307). I. Title II. Series. 746.440941. ISBN 0-7478-0256-4.

ACKNOWLEDGEMENTS
My thanks are due to all the private owners and institutions who have allowed their pieces to be used as illustrations. I am especially grateful to Ann Anderson, Helen Bennett, Xanthe Brooke, Joan Edwards, Sylvia Hogarth, Betty Ring, Sarah Medlam and Naomi Tarrant for their encouragement and advice.

Cover: *Miss Anne Eliza Morritt (1726-97) at her embroidery frame: a portrait by Benjamin West, about 1773-8. (By kind permission of Sir Andrew Morritt.)*

A pastoral scene on a silk ground. A shepherd pipes to an elegantly dressed shepherdess, wearing a jewelled necklace in a country landscape. English, inscribed 'Eliz Tole 1741'. Tole or Toll is a common Bedfordshire name, and she may be Elizabeth Tole who married Thomas Hart at Blunham on 13th October 1757. A variety of stitches in silk and applied seed pearls on satin. (The Lady Lever Art Gallery.)

EIGHTEENTH-CENTURY EMBROIDERY

The Georgian period in Britain began in 1714 with the accession to the throne of the Protestant George I, son of the Electress Sophia of Hanover, descendant of the Stuart king James I (James VI of Scotland). It ended with the death of George IV in 1830.

The bitter religious struggles of the previous century were followed by a long period of political calm in Britain, although there were two abortive attempts by Jacobites in 1715 and 1745 to restore a Catholic Stuart king to the throne. It was a period of peace and prosperity for the upper classes, a time of scientific discoveries and inventions. Crompton's spinning jenny and James Watt's discoveries leading to the steam engine started a momentum towards mechanisation that still continues. It was a period of exploration, when distant countries were discovered and mapped. But during most of the period Britain was at war – against France, and eventually against her own colonies in America, a struggle that resulted in the Declaration of Independence and the foundation of a great nation on the other side of the Atlantic.

During this time, almost imperceptibly, the education of girls became more widespread owing to increased prosperity. Cultivated and intelligent women like the Duchess of Portland and her friend Mrs Delany (1700-88), who were friends of

3

some of the most learned men of their time, were still exceptional, but more women could read and write and middle-class girls were being sent to school, even though their education consisted mostly of accomplishments rather than academic subjects. Needlework was still the main-stay of their instruction, especially needlework that could be displayed, like a picture on the wall. But even the Duch-ess of Portland and Mrs Delany spent much of their time planning and working embroidery for furnishing or dress. The needlework pictures that survive from the eighteenth century reflect the taste of their time as well as the high degree of skill expended upon them.

MATERIALS AND TECHNIQUES
Linen-based panels, canvas work
The fashion for raised work that had flourished in the seventeenth century faded with the new dynasty. But canvas-work, cross stitch and tent stitch (half cross

stitch) worked on evenly woven linen were still the mainstay of most needlewomen's repertoire. Cross stitch was the first stitch worked on a little girl's sampler. Other stitches worked over the counted thread were learned later and could be used to give different effects on a picture. In ad-dition to pictures intended for the wall, the great bulk of pictorial canvas work was produced for furnishing and this is dealt with in a later chapter.

Pictures on a silk ground
The thick white satin of the previous century is rarely found; instead, a finer silk, often backed by linen for strength, appears frequently in schoolgirls' pictures from the 1770s onwards. The design, as before, was taken from a popular en-graving and was sketched on to the silk background, not always by the needlewoman herself. Details such as faces (always difficult to embroider) and hands were usually painted. The clothing

Armchair back: 'Vulcan's Forge'. Vulcan works at his anvil, fashioning the armour for Aeneas, directed by Venus. Behind him, two boys are working at the fire of the forge. The seat shows flowers and a dog. One of a set of twelve chairs, said to be worked by Ann, Lady Mornington (1741-1831), mother of the Duke of Welling-ton. Irish, about 1760.

Detail of the 'Vulcan's Forge' chair back. Silk and wool, tent and cross stitch. The other chairs depict a variety of scenes: Narcissus at the well, a group of dancers, a card game in the open air, and a basket of flowers.

for their lack of originality. It is largely forgotten that the idea that a needlewoman should also create her own designs is a comparatively modern conception, following the teaching of William Morris that the designer and craftsman should be one. This was taken up by the teaching of the Glasgow School of Art, especially of Ann Macbeth, who taught that even children could create simple designs by using lines and circles. However, Ann Macbeth frequently drew designs for others to work, and the firm of William Morris sold designs ready-traced for needlewomen to buy.

and landscape details were worked in smooth silks, with occasional chenille.

Needlepainting

The education of young ladies, like that of their brothers, often included the 'polite art' of drawing and painting. Watercolour sketches of flowers, landscapes and interiors were produced. One or two women, however, succeeded in making full-sized embroidered pictures in varieties of long and short stitch to suggest brush strokes. Working on a firm linen, the needlewoman had a wide range of specially dyed wools to produce the shading required. Usually they were copies of paintings and at the time they were greatly admired, though now they are condemned

Other techniques

Feltwork. Now thought to be a modern technique, appliqué of cut-out shapes in felt or firm woollen cloth was practised towards the end of the eighteenth century. Valances, bed hangings and wall hangings survive, as well as small pictures.

Printwork. Pictures drawn on to a silk or fine linen background were worked in lines of fine black silk to suggest engravings. Occasionally human hair was used to give a sepia tone.

Colifichets. These are of double-faced embroidery worked in smooth silks on paper or vellum. The design was drawn out and the lines pricked so that the needle could pass through without friction.

'The Death of Absalom' (II Samuel 18, 9-14), an American schoolgirl piece, about 1753. Silk embroidery with metal thread on a satin ground . (Centre) Absalom, his hair caught in the branches, hangs from a tree; his mule runs free. (Left) His father, King David, is told of his death. (Right) David playing his harp. There are several versions of this scene in American museums. It has not been found in Britain. (Museum of Fine Arts, Boston.)

BIBLICAL PICTURES

Pictures of biblical scenes do not appear to have been so popular as in the seventeenth century, though Old Testament favourites such as 'The Finding of Moses' continued to be chosen. In the United States of America there are several versions of 'The Death of Absalom' not found in Britain. More scenes from the New Testament were depicted, such as 'Christ Appearing to Mary Magdalen in the Garden' or 'Christ and the Samaritan Woman'. Pictures showing the Virgin are so rare that they are likely to have been the work of Catholic needlewomen.

Surprisingly, a large number of biblical subjects are found on furnishing textiles, screen and chair covers. See the chapter on 'Needlework Furnishings'.

Panel for a firescreen. Silk and wool on canvas. Fine tent stitch with cross-stitch border. The risen Christ appearing to three disciples (John 20, 19). Signed 'HG 1754', with coronet. The initials are those of Henrietta, Duchess of Gordon, whose daughter became the Countess of Wemyss. (The Earl of Wemyss and March, KT.)

A pair of pictures: shepherd and shepherdess. Wool and silk on canvas. A shepherd with sheep, and a shepherdess with a crook and bunch of flowers surrounded with sheep in a flowery landscape. English, inscribed 'Sarah Fletcher 1741'. (Historic Deerfield, Massachusetts.)

PASTORAL SCENES

The taste for biblical scenes that had so absorbed the workers of the seventeenth century was replaced by a passion for the pastoral. The classical authors of Greece and Rome formed the basis of a schoolboy's education. The *Eclogues* of Virgil, celebrating the happiness and innocence of the shepherd's life and the beauty of the countryside, together with his *Georgics*, dealing with agricultural pursuits, were available in translation to their sisters and to those who knew no Greek or Latin. English literature had reflected the pursuit of the pastoral: plays such as Shakespeare's *As You Like It* and Fletcher's *Faithful Shepherdess* were succeeded by the early *Pastorals* of Pope (1709) and Allan Ramsay's *The Gentle Shepherd* (1725).

Most of the pastoral scenes are worked in tent stitch on canvas but some were also executed in silk on a silk foundation. The shepherdesses are elegantly dressed, often with fine jewels. The shepherd also is smartly dressed and often plays a pipe for the delectation of his companion. Only rarely does a note of realism creep in. A panel in the Royal Ontario Museum shows a shepherdess feeding a lamb with milk from a leather bag.

Not surprisingly, this delightful fash-ion was eagerly adopted in colonial America. Much has been discovered by Betty Ring and others about the schools that taught the technique and drew out the engaging scenes.

The 'Boston Fishing Lady' appears on several panels with other couples in a landscape containing sheep, birds, dogs and huntsmen. Nancy Graves Cabot (*Antiques,* July 1941) found no less than twelve panels of this design. The 'Fishing Lady' has not been found in Britain and must be regarded as an American figure. Many of the panels are signed and dated (between 1746 and 1791). Some are 'chimney pieces', enclosed in a handsome walnut frame with gilt moulding to hang over the fireplace.

As with the biblical pictures, these pastoral scenes were not drawn out by the needlewoman herself. Pattern drawers were employed by haberdashers who sold the materials, linen, silks and wools in London, and advertisements have been found in Boston newspapers in America. In 1738 a Mrs Condy advertised in the *Boston Weekly News Letter*:
'To be had at Mrs Condy's near the Old North Meeting House: All sorts of beautiful figures on Canvas, for Tent Stick; the Patterns from London, but drawn by her

7

Left: *A shepherdess feeding a lamb. Tent stitch and geometrical satin stitch on linen. A shepherdess, elegantly dressed with necklace and hat, crook and dog at her side, feeds a lamb from a leather bottle. English, inscribed 'EH 1730'. (The Royal Ontario Museum.)*

Below: *'The Boston Fishing Lady', worked by Eunice Bourne, wife of Colonel Sylvanus Bourne, Barnstable, Massachusetts, 1740-60. This wide panel, intended as a 'chimney piece', is similar to several others. They are thought to have been first drawn out by Mrs Condy, a schoolteacher in Boston. Some of the figures, notably the couple on the right, derive from engravings, but the Fishing Lady herself is still unidentified and remains distinctively American. Fine tent stitch in silk and wool with metal thread on linen. (Museum of Fine Arts, Boston.)*

much cheaper than English drawing; All sorts of Canvas without drawing, also Silk Shades, Slacks, Floss, Cruells of all sorts, the best White Chapple Needles, and every thing for all Sorts of Work.'

Mrs Condy (1686-1747) was the wife of a schoolmaster and opened her own school, possibly after she was widowed in 1741. She is believed to have been the originator of the 'Fishing Lady' panels. She continued to draw out designs and advertised in March 1742:

'Mrs Condy opens her school next Week, and persons may be supplied with the Materials for the Works she teaches, whether they learn of her or not. She draws patterns of all sorts, especially Pocket Books, House Wives, Screens, Pictures, Chimney Pieces, Settees and Chairs, Escrutores etc., for *Tent Stitch* in a plainer Manner and cheaper than those which come from London.'

Mrs Condy died in 1747 and a month after her death her daughter advertised: 'A Variety of very beautiful Patterns to draw by, of the late Mrs Susannah Condy, deceas'd, any Gentlewoman or others disposed to improve and purchase which will be very much to their advantage, may inquire of Elizabeth Russell, Daughter of the decease'd...'

Other schools flourished in Boston and New England, as well as other areas. This work, which has a gaiety and spontaneity not so common in Britain, has been identified, so that the work of individual schools can be recognised. Little is yet known of comparable schools in Britain, though many of the pieces that survive were worked by schoolgirls and must have been drawn out by the mistress or someone on her staff. Several pieces of the 1760s are marked 'Worked at Mrs Rosco's Boarding School, Bristol'. An Edinburgh sampler dated 1745 is inscribed 'At Mrs Seton's'. Mrs Seton had a school in Edinburgh, but little is known about her and so far only two samplers have been found.

Adults, or those working at home, had to rely on artists who were not too proud to draw out designs: even William Blake made a drawing of gentle hares for the wife of a friend to embroider. Otherwise, they obtained their designs from the haberdasher who supplied their materials: canvas, silks and crewels. Some offered patterns ready drawn by a pattern-drawer, described somewhat cynically in *The London Tradesman* (1747), a guide to careers and prospects:
'Pattern-drawers are employed in drawing Patterns for Callico-Printers, for Embroiderers, Lace-Workers, Quilters, and several little branches belonging to Women's Apparel. They draw patterns on paper... They draw shapes and Figures upon Men's Waistcoats to be embroidered, upon Women's Petticoats, and other wearing-Apparel, for all of which they have large prices. This requires a fruitful Fancy, to invent new whims to please the changeable Foible of the Ladies, for whose use their work is chiefly intended. It requires no great taste in Painting, nor in the Principles of Drawing, but wild kind of Imagination, to adorn their works with a sort of regular Confusion, to attract the eye but not please the Judgement; though if he has a Painter's Head, and a natural Turn for designing, his Works must have more of Nature, and cannot fail to please better than the wild Scrawls of a mechanical Drawer.'

Since few pattern-drawers were skilled in figure drawing, they relied upon well-drawn engravings, from which they took not only the figures but often the whole composition. Schoolteachers also used engravings as models for embroideries. Many of these engravings have been identified.

'The Harvest' (chair cover). British, first half of the eighteenth century. A more realistic view of the labour of country life, probably taken from an engraving. Cross stitch and fine tent stitch on linen. (Mrs Dundas-Bekker.)

Ferdinand and Miranda, from Shakespeare's 'The Tempest', in an oval frame with a label on the back inscribed 'ELIZABETH DURRANT finished this piece of needlework from the design of ANGELICA, Tempest Act III Sc.4 at Miss Adam's School, Lewes, Sussex 7 Nov. 1791'. Painted faces and hands, silk straight stitches and French knots on silk. See the engraving by Angelica Kauffman on page 11. (James Claydon Esq.)

THEATRICAL AND LITERARY SCENES

The taste for pastoral romance appeared to fade after the middle of the eighteenth century. More dramatic scenes from the classics, the stage, and romantic novels began to appear, reflecting the widening of the education of young ladies. Geography and 'the use of globes' are all reflected in the choice of needlework.

Scenes from the plays of Shakespeare were popular and ensured that the story at least became familiar, and a flood of prints taken from the works of well-known artists offered designs for pictures carefully embroidered on a silk background. The faces and other details were often painted in watercolour. Angelica Kauffman (1741-1807), a Swiss artist who lived in London between 1766 and 1781 and was a friend of Sir Joshua Reynolds, painted classical historical and literary scenes which were widely admired. Her paintings, and those of other artists, were reproduced as engravings that were framed and hung on walls or used as designs for needlework.

In 1791 Elizabeth Durrant completed an oval picture of Ferdinand and Miranda from *The Tempest* by Shakespeare at the school of Miss Adams at Lewes, East Sussex. She inscribed all the details on the back of the frame in elegant script on a shield-shaped label, including the name of the artist: 'Angelica'. The same year, a schoolgirl in Dublin also worked a picture of Ferdinand and Miranda, but taken from a painting by G. B. Cipriani (1727-85), published by Boydell in 1788. What is remarkable about this needlework picture, however, is that she completed no less than four, on each of which she inscribed not only the date on which it was completed, but also the date on which she commenced it:

'1. Eliza Farran began to work Charlotte at the Tomb of Werter the 10th of May & finished it the 4th of July 1790.
2. Eliza Farran began to work Griselda returning to her Father the 28th of Jan & finished it the 1st of March 1791.

10

An engraving of Ferdinand and Miranda, after Angelica Kauffman, by P. W. Tomkins, published by J. Birchall, London, 1786. 'If you sit down, I'll bear your logs the while. Pray give me that, I'll carry't to the pile.' See Elizabeth Durrant's picture, page 10. (British Museum.)

Ferdinand and Miranda, from 'The Tempest'. Miranda stands with her father, Prospero, looking at Ferdinand. Caliban lurks behind, while Ariel flies above. Silk picture with painted faces worked by Eliza Farran, Dublin, 1791. The design is taken from an engraving by Bartholozzi after a painting by G. B. Cipriani, published in 1788. (Miss Ann Parkinson.)

The label on the back of the frame – 'Eliza Farran began to work Ferdinand and Miranda the 18th of March and finished it the 2nd of May 1791' – with the label of the framer, Jackson, Essex Bridge, Dublin. (Miss Ann Parkinson.)

3. Eliza Farran began to work Ferdinand and Miranda the 18th of March & finished it the 2nd May 1791.
4. Eliza Farran began to work Lord Thomas and Fair Elinor the 2nd of December 1791 & finished the 6 Feb 1792.' (A ballad in Percy's *Reliques,*1765. Thomas Percy became Bishop of Dromore.)

It is not known which school in Dublin Eliza Farran attended but she was given a useful introduction to literature. Her pictures were all framed by the firm of Jackson, 5 Essex Bridge, Dublin, who had been in business since the 1740s. She married in 1806 William Colvill of Newtownards and Dublin and had a son, a professional soldier, who was lost at Scutari during the Crimean War, and a daughter, whose descendants still cherish Eliza's pictures. In Boston, Massachusetts, a meticulously worked silk picture of a scene from *The Tempest* was executed by Caroline Blaney about 1810. This shows Miranda with Prospero and Caliban and is thought to have been painted on to the silk by John Johnston, a celebrated Boston portraitist, after an engraving by Fuseli.

The romantic poems of Sir Walter Scott also offered inspiration. Scenes from *The Lady of the Lake* (1810) are found in the Lady Lever Art Gallery and the Royal Museum of Scotland. Two other versions of the same scene, Fair Ellen in a boat on Loch Katrine, survive in the United States. These two are believed to have been drawn by Godfrey Folwell (1799-1855), who advertised in the *Philadelphia Directory* as 'G. Folwell, teacher of Fancy Drawing'.

An occasional biblical scene is found in this technique, such as 'The Finding of Moses', with Pharaoh's daughter and her attendants wearing fashionable high-waisted neo-classical muslin gowns.

'The Lady of the Lake': a scene from the narrative poem by Sir Walter Scott, published in 1810. Ellen, in a boat on Loch Katrine, with probably Roderick Dhu, the Highland chief in love with her. An almost identical version is in the Lady Lever Art Gallery. Worked in silks on silk, with knotted stitches for foliage. The faces are painted. (The Royal Museum of Scotland.)

'The Finding of Moses' (Exodus 2, 3-10). Silk and wool on silk with faces and other details in watercolour. English, about 1800. Pharaoh's daughter and her ladies wear high-waisted gowns, and the Pyramids are depicted in the midst of a leafy landscape. (The Lady Lever Art Gallery.)

Charlotte at the tomb of Werther. Inscribed on the back: 'Eliza Farran began to work Charlotte at the Tomb of Werter the 10th of May & finished it the 4th of July 1790'. (Miss Ann Parkinson.)

The Muse of Poetry paying homage to Shakespeare. English, 1782-1800. Several examples of this silk embroidery survive, all faithfully following the engraving by Bartholozzi (1782) after a drawing by Angelica Kauffman. The engraving is also believed to have inspired the family memorial embroideries that became a fashion in the United States from 1800 to 1830. (The Lady Lever Art Gallery.)

MEMORIAL PICTURES

Angelica Kauffman's painting 'The Muse of Poetry Paying Homage to Shakespeare' was published as an engraving in 1782. This romantic scene, with the female figure dropping flowers over a tomb bearing a carved medallion labelled 'SHAKESPEARE', served as a model for several known embroidered pictures (Victoria and Albert Museum, Lady Lever Art Gallery and Mellerstain, Berwickshire). In Dublin Eliza Farran's first needlework picture shows Charlotte mourning over the classical tomb of Werther, from Goethe's romance *The Trials of Young Werther* (1774). Other needlework versions of this scene survive. Admiral Nelson, a national hero, is commemorated in two needlework pictures at the Lady Lever Art Gallery, one taken from a portrait print.

These are general expressions of romantic sorrow, however. Personal or fam-ily mourning seems hardly to have been celebrated in needlework in Britain during the Georgian period, though a remarkable and enigmatic piece appeared in the saleroom, signed 'EP 1746'. It shows three grieving women in different-coloured gowns, overlooking three beds hung with mourning draperies. The beds contain four corpses, possibly of children. Nothing is known of its background or history. It is a dignified scene of family grief in an age of high infant mortality.

In the United States the death of George Washington in 1799 initiated a wave of memorial pictures that have no counterpart in Britain. Prints of the hero were produced in the United States and in Britain. They offered designs for embroidery, to be worked by young ladies under supervision of a schoolmistress, and many survive. However, this was speedily fol-

Left: *Charlotte mourning over the grave of Werther. Silk embroidery on blue woollen background. English, 1790-1800. Goethe's romance 'The Trials of Young Werther' was published in 1774. It inspired many needlework pictures. (The Leicester Museums.)*

Right: *Admiral Nelson, memorial portrait, English, painted silk, worked with silks and chenille, 1805. The figure appears to have been taken from a mezzotint of 1799 after a portrait by L. F. Abbot, but the motto of his famous signal at the battle of Trafalgar in 1805 shows that the needlework was drawn out after that date. (The Lady Lever Art Gallery.)*

Memorial picture signed 'EP 1746'. This mysterious and skilfully worked panel shows three women, all young, one in yellow with a handkerchief, one in red with a printed paper, the third in dark blue carrying flowers. They gaze down at three white-draped beds adorned with cherub heads and a skull and crossbones, with hourglasses beside them. In one bed two small heads can be seen; the other two each contain a dead child. Beside them stand a boy with a sheep and a girl with a dog. English. Tent and cross stitch on canvas. (Phillips, Fine Art Auctioneers.)

lowed by the widespread fashion for a more personal memorial for a member of the family of the needlewoman. One of the earliest appears to be that of Lucretia Carew, 1800, now at the Museum of Stoney Brook, New York. Exquisitely worked on silk, it shows Lucretia's family, her parents and lame brother with crutches, all in black, at the classical tomb, shaded by a weeping willow, of her sister, who died in childbirth in 1800. Lucretia's mother had a school, and it was no doubt done under her supervision. Other schools followed the fashion. They gave employment to local artists, who drew out the designs and in many cases painted the faces, and to local frame-makers, who usually mounted the pictures under black and gold glass mats.

So many of these pictures survive, with their black-clad mourners at classical tombs beneath weeping willow trees, that it is clear the fashion spread all over New England and the other states.

Washington memorial. Just as the death of Nelson inspired memorial pictures in Britain, so the death of George Washington in 1799 began a spate of silk-embroidered mourning panels in the United States. This anonymous example was worked in Boston, 1805-15, and is thought to have been painted on the silk by the portrait painter John Johnston. (Betty Ring.)

Inscribed 'Wrought by Nancy Torrey 1809'. The mourning family stands at the tomb of Caleb Torrey, who died in 1808, the father of Nancy (1793-1869). The figures are entirely painted; the two urns are embroidered in gold thread. Worked at the school of Miss Abby Wright of South Hadley, Massachusetts. A family memorial picture of the type worked in girls' schools in the United States. (Betty Ring.)

Left: 'The Old Gardener'. Needlepainting by Miss Anne Eliza Morritt, dated 1769. Shaded wools in long stitches, suggesting brush strokes. (Sir Andrew Morritt.)
Right: Needlework self-portrait of Mrs Knowles, showing her at her frame working at the portrait of George III after Zoffany. (By gracious permission of Her Majesty the Queen.)

NEEDLEPAINTING

As the eighteenth century progressed, the education of young ladies perceptibly widened to include literature and poetry, reflected in their choice of subject for needlework, still the mainstay of a girl's upbringing. But throughout the Georgian period there were strong-minded women of formidable intelligence who educated themselves to the level of their brothers but who had no outlet for their talents except in conversation and the friendship of learned men. Mrs Delany, the friend of Dean Swift, and her friend, Margaret Cavendish Harley, Duchess of Portland, were able to indulge, as widows, their passion for botany and natural history. Mrs Delany embroidered throughout her long life but was renowned for her meticulous cut-paper delineations of flowers, now in the British Museum. Only the exceptional woman, like Angelica Kauffman, whose career as an artist was fostered by her father, could compete with men on equal terms. Others used their skill in embroidery to produce pictures in the style of well-known paintings.

The earliest appears to have been Miss Anne Eliza Morritt (1726-97). She was the eldest daughter of a Yorkshire landowner. Her father bought what is now the Treasurer's House in York as a town house, which she and her sisters continued to inhabit after the purchase of Rokeby Park in County Durham by her brother in 1769. It is not known if she was the originator of this style of needlepainting in crewels: she signed one of her panels 'A. E. Morritt Acu pinxit 1756' (that is, painted with the needle). The term had been used in the seventeenth century for the realistic designs of flowers and saints worked in smooth silks on vestments in French convents.

Miss Morritt's subjects were taken from paintings in the house: romantic landscapes with waterfalls; a panel of birds, pheasants, chickens and ducklings by M. Craddock (1660-1717), from which she took details and rendered faithfully the plumage and bright eyes, the stitches following the brush strokes of the painted panel. Later she followed more famous models: Rubens, the fashionable Salvator Rosa and Zuccarelli. Her portrait (see front cover), painted by Benjamin West when she was about fifty, shows her, needle in hand, at her frame, with a picture before her. This is Andrea Sacci's 'Vision of St Romuald' in the Vatican, which presumably she took from an engraving. She was later to work a panel showing her own head from West's portrait. She was, indeed, exceedingly skilled in depicting faces and hands. There is a masterly 'Head of Bacchus' and a small oval of her younger brother, Bacon, who died early, taken from a portrait still at Rokeby.

Her sisters lived with her at York. Frances, some ten years younger, appears also to have been highly educated, described by their nephew, J. B. S. Morritt, an early traveller to the Near East, as 'an advocate for petticoat independence' with 'strange notions... about the advantages of travel for ladies'. It was Frances who lent him a scholarly book by Jean Baptiste Chevallier, published by the Royal Society of Edinburgh in 1791, and which he describes as 'as great an incentive to my touring as any I had read'. He sent her lively and affectionate letters describing the site of Troy, with classical references needing no explanation.

Miss Morritt did not exhibit her needlework pictures publicly, but they became well-known to those who visited York and were received by the sisters. The traveller Arthur Young, in *A Six Months' Tour through the North of England* (1779), recorded: 'By far the most curious things to be seen in York are the copies of several capital paintings, worked by Miss Morret, a lady of most surprising genius.' A Scottish traveller in 1775 wrote that, after visiting the Roman remains in York, he and his companions sent their compliments to the Miss Morritts and went to see 'the extraordinary sewed work'. The whole room was hung about with the pictures in gilt frames. Miss Morritt died in 1797.

Her epitaph in Selby Abbey hints that her life was not entirely placid:
'Blest shade while GENIUS in thy earlier days
Fired thee to emulate the pencils praise
To seize the painters powers without the name
And soar on female attributes to fame
This verse records how to these powers were join'd
The strongest, manliest energies of mind.
Records those years of pain thy fame sustain'd
With patience firm, with love and faith unfeign'd
And hope that ever hovering o'er thy head
The brilliant palm of bliss eternal spread.'

She continued to embroider to the end. Her last picture, 'Cock and Hen', is dated 1796, the year before she died. Her embroidered pictures, some forty-seven, are preserved at Rokeby Park, the home of her brother and his descendants.

Mrs Knowles (1733-1807), the 'fair Quakeress', also worked panels in worsteds after well-known paintings. She is, however, better remembered for her friendship with Dr Johnson, who wrote to Mrs Thrale, another learned lady, in 1776: 'There was Mrs Knowles, that works the sutile pictures... ' 'Sutile' means stitched or sewn, but, by using a long s, this has been read as 'futile pictures', indicating a contempt that Dr Johnson certainly did not intend to convey. Indeed, he had a warm admiration for her.

She was born Mary Morris of Quaker parents in Rugeley, Staffordshire. Eager and intelligent, she painted, wrote and designed a garden for Sampson Lloyd, the banker, at Birmingham. In 1761 she married Dr Thomas Knowles, a wealthy Quaker physician, one of the Committee of Six organised by the Quakers to oppose slavery. They had one son, George, born in 1773. Dr Knowles died in 1784.

She was introduced to Queen Charlotte in 1771 by a fellow Quaker, the artist Benjamin West, whose work George III

greatly admired. The Queen invited her to copy in needlework a portrait of the king painted by Zoffany. Mrs Knowles completed it the same year, and thus began a friendship with the royal pair, with visits to Buckingham House, wearing her simple Quaker dress. She embroidered a self-portrait in 1779, showing her in demure cap and fichu, with the portrait of George III on the frame. This may be her second version of the Zoffany portrait, now in the Victoria and Albert Museum.

Unlike Miss Morritt, she did not leave a large legacy of embroidered pictures. Indeed, her contemporaries did not regard her merely as an embroideress. A letter written at the time of her death in 1807 is preserved in the library of the Society of Friends: 'Poor Mrs Knowles! She is also among the inhabitants of Eternity. I attended her remains to Bunhill Fields [the Quaker burial ground]. She was a woman of extraordinary Endowments, and I think her name will be accompanied by some celebrity in the an-

nals of literary Ladies...'

The most renowned of all needlepainters of the Georgian period, whose fame lasted into the Victorian era, was Miss Mary Linwood. She was born in Birmingham in 1756, one of a large family. Her father lost his money, with the result that the family moved to Leicester in 1764, where her mother, Mrs Hannah Linwood, opened a boarding school for young ladies at the Priory, Belgrave Gate, now demolished. Mary was carefully educated in literature, painting, music and needlework.

In 1776 she and her mother exhibited needlework pictures at the Society of Artists in London. The following year another of Mary's pictures was accepted. In 1789 she copied in worsteds the painting 'Salvator Mundi' by Carlo Dolci, in the collection of the Earl of Exeter. He offered to buy it, but she refused to sell, and at the end of her long life bequeathed it to 'the Reigning Sovereign of Great Britain and Ireland, as an heirloom of the Crown'.

She continued to complete large canvases after well-known paintings, working on a firm linen tammy with worsted dyed to her specifications. In 1798 she had sufficient panels to open an exhibition at Hanover Square, London. This went on tour to Edinburgh, Glasgow, Belfast, Dublin and Limerick. On its return, it was shown in rooms in Leicester Square, London, where it was displayed with skill, the main hall hung with 'scarlet cloth, satin and silver'. A version of Northcote's 'Lady Jane Grey Visited by the Abbot and Keeper of the Throne at Night' was shown in a prison cell at the end of a dark passage. Gainsborough's painting of 'A Woodman in a Storm' was reproduced full size, about 6 feet (1.8 metres) high. The actual painting was destroyed by fire in 1810, so this is the only representation. It now hangs in the Newarke Houses, belonging to the Leicester Museums.

She embroidered two portraits of Napoleon and in 1803 visited Paris, where Bonaparte invited her to dinner and conferred upon her the freedom of Paris. She had been received by Queen Charlotte and the princesses, but not on the easy footing of Mrs Delany or Mrs Knowles, possibly because she continued to live in Leicester.

Her mother died in 1804, and Miss Linwood continued with the school, which lasted until 1843, two years before her death at the age of ninety. The exhibition of 'Pictures in Worsted', which had formed one of the attractions of London for nearly half a century, also closed on her death. She had offered the collection of some hundred of her pictures to the British Museum, and then to the House of Lords. Both offers were refused, and the pictures were sold for less than £1000.

Miss Linwood wrote *The Leicestershire Tales* in four volumes (1808), an opera and a sacred oratorio. Her portrait, painted at the height of her powers, shows her not as a needlewoman at her frame like Miss Morritt and Mrs Knowles, but as an artist, pencil in hand, with a portfolio under her arm. Her name is still remembered in Leicester. A statue has been erected, and a school has been named after her.

Other needlewomen mastered this exacting technique. Three examples hang at Burghley House, Stamford, Lincolnshire.

Needlepainting: a goldfinch starved to death in a cage; signed 'M. Linwood', after John Russell RA (1745-1806), the pastellist.
> Thanks, gentle maid, for all my woes,
> And thanks for this effectual close
> And cure of every ill!
> Mere cruelty could none express;
> And I, if you had shewn me less,
> Had been your prisoner still.

(The Leicester Museums.)

Wall hanging signed 'Anne Grant 1750': a tiled conservatory with yellow background. Anne Grant was the sister of the agricultural reformer Sir Francis Grant of Monymusk, Aberdeenshire. Tent stitch in silk and wool on canvas. (Sir Archibald Grant of Monymusk.)

NEEDLEWORK FURNISHINGS

Surprisingly, much of the pictorial embroidery worked during the Georgian period was not made to be framed and hung on the wall but embellished textile furnishings, particularly screens, large wall hangings and seat covers. This was in addition to the characteristic 'chimney pieces' of pastoral scenes found in New England.

Wall hangings, often imitating woven tapestries, still survive, notably those made in the 1730s for Stoke Edith, a house destroyed by fire, which are now at Montacute House, Somerset (National Trust). These show sunny garden scenes, with an outdoor meal. Another, at Monymusk, Aberdeenshire, shows a conservatory with plants and is dated 1750. At Wallington, a National Trust house in Northumberland, tent-stitch panels worked by Lady Julia Calverley have a

floral design, but her sixfold screen, signed 'Julia Calverley 1727', depicts lively scenes taken from a variety of sources, including illustrations by Franz Cleyn from Ogilby's editions of Virgil published in 1659.

Ornamental firescreens became fashionable around the middle of the eighteenth century. They were intended to stand in front of the empty fireplace during the summer, when no fires were lit, so that a decorative textile – silk, tapestry or needlework – could be placed there without damage to the rectangular frame. Embroidered panels sometimes displayed biblical or theatrical scenes instead of the more common flowers or birds. A firescreen in the Victoria and Albert Museum shows an actor, Angelo Constantini, a member of an Italian troupe who played in Paris in 1688, taken from a popular

Left: *Two panels from a sixfold screen, signed 'Julia Calverley 1727'. (Left top) The drunken Silenus; (bottom) the vintage. (Right top) A piper with Harlequin and a lady and gentleman; (bottom) an old man smoking, a girl with a basket on her head. The scenes derive from a variety of prints. Lady Julia also completed ten wall panels dated 1717 in three and a half years, and a set of chair covers. All are now at Wallington Hall, Northumberland. (The National Trust for England and Wales.)*

Right: *Firescreen: a monkey holding fruit in a landscape within a scrolled frame with flowers; signed 'JD 1766'. The initials are those of Janet Dalrymple, sister of Lord Hailes. She was born in 1730 and died unmarried in 1784. Scottish. Very fine tent stitch on linen. (Lady Antonia Dalrymple.)*

French theatrical print engraved by Jean Mariette. Two firescreens worked by Henrietta, Duchess of Gordon, survive. One, left to her youngest son, Lord Adam Gordon, shows 'The Sacrifice of Isaac' and is now at the Palace of Holyroodhouse in Edinburgh. It derives from a large biblical engraving published by N. Visscher in Amsterdam about 1660. The other, signed and dated 'HG 1754', belonged to her daughter, the Countess of Wemyss, and shows the risen Christ appearing to his disciples. Since the panel was often the same size as a rectangular chair back, the same design could be used for either. Indeed, at Newhailes, Midlothian, there are a chair cover and a firescreen taken

from the same Parisian engraving of about 1690, titled 'Le Printemps', but in each the figure of Spring wears a dress of different colours.

Card tables. Card games were an immensely popular diversion in the eighteenth century. Fortunes were lost or won. Card tables usually had tops covered in green baize, but embroidered covers were also used, depicting flowers or a pastoral scene. Several show a game in progress with counters and must have been distracting to play on.

Seat covers. Chairs, settees and stools remain one of the richest sources of eighteenth-century pictorial needlework. Sets of a dozen chairs were embroidered, the

Above: *Detail (left) of another panel of the Wallington screen (see page 23), illustrating a swarm of bees and based on the engraving (right) by W. Hollar after a design by Franz Cleyn, an illustration in Book IV of Virgil's 'Georgics', published by John Ogilby in 1641. (Left: The National Trust for England and Wales.)*

Firescreen inscribed 'Elizabeth Newdigate 1754 aged 84'. She was Elizabeth Twisden, the second wife of Sir Richard Newdigate, third Baronet of Arbury. Coloured silks on a dark brown ground. (Viscount Daventry.)

24

Right: *Chair cover: 'The Judgement of Solomon'. The chair back is upholstered with the scene from I Kings 3, 16-28, taken from an engraving after Rubens. The seat has a scene from the Parable of the Prodigal Son. One of a set of eight chairs entirely covered with scenes from the Old and New Testaments. English, about 1760. Tent stitch in wool and silk. (The Lady Lever Art Gallery.)*

Below: *'The Judgement of Solomon', engraved by S. A. Bolswerte after Peter Paul Rubens, in a volume of Bible illustrations by Nicholas Visscher, published in Amsterdam about 1660. (The British Museum.)*

Card-table top: one of a pair, both unused. The game of quadrille, a four-handed version of ombre, is laid out with counters. Other table tops with cards laid out still survive in Britain and the United States. Tent stitch and cross stitch on canvas. (The Earl of Wemyss and March, KT.)

Stool top. The cover, worked in silk on canvas, shows a straw hat with blue ribbon, a feather and an almanac for 1757. One of a set of seven stools worked by Sophia Conyers (1718-74), the first wife of Sir Roger Newdigate, fifth Baronet. (Viscount Daventry.)

Chair seat, showing a countryman with a rabbit on a staff, and a girl with a basket of flowers on her head, surrounded by a flower border on a yellow ground. The girl derives from an engraving after Jacques Stella called 'Pastorale no. 12, Le Soir', used as a source for many embroideries on both sides of the Atlantic, and for woven tapestries. One of a set of four chair covers, two now at Winterthur, Delaware, and two at Boston, Massachusetts. (The Henry Francis du Pont Winterthur Museum.)

pictorial backs often showing a cheerful mix of pastoral, biblical and classical scenes enclosed in a matching wreath to give unity to the set. The figures are mostly confined to the back, as there was a convention, not always observed, that one did not sit on people. This convention is totally disregarded in a remarkable set of eight chairs in the Lady Lever Art Gallery, which have backs and seats entirely covered with scenes from the Old and New Testaments. Two are taken from engravings after Rubens.

Not all needlewomen of the period took their designs from printed sources, however. A set of seven stools with silk-embroidered tops survives at Arbury Hall, Warwickshire. They were worked by

Sophia Conyers (1718-74), the first wife of Sir Roger Newdigate. It is said that she asked her husband what design she should choose and he told her to work what lay upon them. The result is a series of delightful *trompe l'oeil* embroideries. One shows a workbag, knotting shuttle and silks. Another shows her straw hat with blue ribbon, a feather and an almanac for 1757, a third a brace of pheasants.

In America also, as the advertisements of Mrs Condy and others make clear, pictorial as well as floral designs could be drawn out on canvas for furnishings. Four engaging chair covers, now divided between Winterthur (Delaware) and Boston, show country figures enclosed in a yellow floral border.

27

Sketch of two wall panels of cut felt, tinted with watercolour, applied to yellow woollen ribbed material (moreen), worked by Lady Mary Hog about 1793 for the drawing room of Newliston House, West Lothian. The other spaces were filled with similar panels. The house was designed by Robert Adam. (Sir John Soane's Museum, London.)

OTHER TECHNIQUES

Feltwork

This is now regarded as a modern technique, but examples of felt appliqué with embroidered details survive from the 1790s. Most remarkable are a set of wall hangings at Newliston, West Lothian, made in the style of Robert Adam, who designed the house in 1791 for Thomas Hog. The panels were worked by his wife, Lady Mary Hog, who originally made fourteen panels, of which nine survive. The cut-out shapes are applied to yellow moreen, a widely used woollen furnishing material with a watered surface, and have highlights of watercolour paint and silk embroidery.

Lady Mary also worked a set of bed hangings, now in the Georgian House, Edinburgh (National Trust for Scotland), in the same technique. This is a much simpler and more rapid design of a ribbon

Collage of flowers: coloured felt cut and applied to a linen background. On the reverse is a label inscribed: 'Made in 1790 by Elizabeth Catherine Sleath, wife of James Whiting Yorke of Walmersgate'. The flowers are typical of the mid eighteenth century: moss roses, introduced in 1735, the popular show auriculas, and a passion flower. Identical feltwork pictures survive, suggesting this was a kit. (Lady Victoria Wemyss.)

28

DURHAM CATHEDRAL from above THE NEW BRIDGE

'Durham Cathedral from above the New Bridge': fine black silk stitches on silk to represent an engraving. English, about 1800. (The Royal Museum of Scotland.)

swag with flowers and leaves on cream moreen. Each petal and leaf is the same shape, attached by widely spaced silk stitches. The applied material is not felt but a firmly woven fabric with a nap, possibly broadcloth. Other furnishing pieces of the same period in this technique are known. In addition, three small pictures exist showing a basket of flowers with a butterfly, all consisting of the same components but arranged differently, according to the taste of the needlewoman. It would seem that they were bought ready-cut as kits. Two were made in Scotland, one in England. No doubt others will emerge.

Printwork

Before the invention of photography multiple illustrations were disseminated by either woodcuts or engravings. Engravings were made by gouging lines on a metal plate with a pointed tool, a burin. The addition of dots that increased the

light and shade enabled black and white reproductions of paintings to become freely available. They became immensely popular in the second half of the eighteenth century, decorating the walls of rooms and popularising the works of well-known painters.

These engravings, as we have seen, were widely used as designs for embroidered pictures, which are sometimes called printwork. The term should be reserved, however, for the type of embroidery that imitated the fine black lines, the dots and cross-hatching of a print. Many of these, worked around 1790 to 1820, show small landscapes and are worked entirely in black silk on a cream ground. Some of the finer details may be worked in human hair, to give a sepia tone.

Ribbon work

Ribbons for embellishing dress were available in great variety. Very narrow ribbons that could be threaded through a

'A View of Godalming Church, Surrey': black silk embroidery on a white (now yellowed) silk ground with watercolour highlights. (Guildford Museum.)

Flower piece, one of a pair, said to be firescreens, worked by Frances Dixon, 1785; poppy, lilac and pansy. The other shows moss rose, pea and lily of the valley. Silk embroidery, chenille with chiffon flowers. (The Laing Museum, Newcastle upon Tyne.)

needle with a wide eye were occasionally used to enliven a flower piece, worked upon fine material that did not offer too much resistance when pulled through, though the hole could be enlarged by the use of a stiletto. Occasionally the flower piece is given added realism by introducing leaves or petals of fine silk gauze. The fragility of such pieces caused them to disintegrate, so that they are now rarely found.

Tambour work

Tambour work is a technique introduced to Europe from India in the 1760s. Fine material, such as muslin, was stretched over a round frame (French *tambour* = drum) and a continuous line was worked by means of a hook, which pulled up the thread held below. The resulting loops made a fine chain stitch, which could be made more rapidly than with a needle. It became an elegant accomplishment for ladies, who kept the tools and threads in decorated workbags. It was also used in French workrooms for decorating gentlemen's waistcoats and other garments. It was introduced into Scotland in 1782 to embellish the fine white muslin made there. Because it produced a continuous line, it was suitable only for small flower pieces as pictures.

Colifichets

Colifichets are double-faced silk embroidery on paper or vellum. The French word meant a trifle. This extremely exacting technique, which probably originated in China, was practised by nuns and was not, therefore, taught to British girls except those sent abroad for a Catholic education. The two daughters of the Earl of Traquair, aged seventeen and eighteen, were sent to a Paris convent to 'finish' their education in 1713. The following year Lady Anne Stuart wrote to her mother: 'There is not a monstray in Paris wherein they teach more kinds of needleworks...As for works, we have learned the coly fishes, and to make purses...' The 'coly fishes' they learned, as well as the purses, are still in their Scottish home: two flower pieces and two religious subjects, framed between two sheets of glass, so that the meticulous stitchery on both sides can be seen.

Others attempted the technique. Miss Morritt was one who did, and her framed flower piece is preserved at Rokeby with the other pictures.

Colifichet, a double-faced embroidery on paper, worked in silks and metal thread: a Chalice and Host, beneath crowned draperies. Worked by one of the two elder daughters, Anne or Lucy, of the fourth Earl of Traquair in 1714 in the Ursuline convent of St Jacques in Paris, where the girls had been sent to finish their education. (Mrs Flora Maxwell Stuart of Traquair.)

31

FURTHER READING

Brett, K. B. *English Embroidery*. Royal Ontario Museum, 1972.
Brooke, Xanthe. *Catalogue of Embroideries*. The Lady Lever Art Gallery, 1992.
Clabburn, Pamela. *The Needleworker's Dictionary*. Macmillan, 1976.'
Ring, Betty. *Schoolgirl Embroidery, American Samplers and Pictorial Needlework*. A. Knopf, 1993.
Swain, Margaret. *Figures on Fabric*. A. & C. Black, 1980.
Swain, Margaret. *Scottish Embroidery*. Batsford, 1986.
Warner, Pamela. *Embroidery, A History*. Batsford, 1991.

PLACES TO VISIT

It is always advisable to write or telephone in advance of a visit, especially to country houses, with limited opening times. Needlework pictures of the eighteenth century are not highly regarded by museum curators and are unlikely to be on display in the public galleries.

UNITED KINGDOM
Arbury Hall, Nuneaton, Warwickshire CV10 7PT. Telephone: 01203 382804.
The Bowes Museum, Barnard Castle, County Durham DL12 8NP. Telephone: 01833 690606.
Burghley House, Stamford, Lincolnshire PE9 3JY. Telephone: 01780 52451.
Fitzwilliam Museum, Trumpington Street, Cambridge CB2 1RB. Telephone: 01223 332900.
Guildford Museum, Castle Arch, Quarry Street, Guildford, Surrey GU1 3SX. Telephone: 01483 444750.
Lady Lever Art Gallery, Port Sunlight Village, Wirral, Merseyside L62 5EQ. Telephone: 0151-645 3623.
Laing Art Gallery, Higham Place, Newcastle upon Tyne, Tyne and Wear NE1 8AG. Telephone: 0191-232 6989 or 7734.
Newliston House, Kirkliston, West Lothian EH29 9EB. Telephone: 0131-333 3231.
Rokeby Park, Barnard Castle, County Durham DL12 9RZ. Telephone: 01833 27268.
Royal Museum of Scotland, Chambers Street, Edinburgh EH1 1JF. Telephone: 0131-225 7534.
Sion Hill Hall, Kirby Wiske, Thirsk, North Yorkshire YO7 4EU. Telephone: 01845 587206.
Traquair House, Innerleithen, Peeblesshire EH44 6PW. Telephone: 01896 830323 or 830785.
Victoria and Albert Museum, Cromwell Road, South Kensington, London SW7 2RL. Telephone: 0171-938 8500.
Wallington, Cambo, Morpeth, Northumberland NE61 4AR. Telephone: 01670 74283.
York Castle Museum, Tower Street, York YO1 1RY. Telephone: 01904 653611.

CANADA
Royal Ontario Museum, 100 Queen's Park, Toronto, Ontario M5C 2C6.

UNITED STATES OF AMERICA
Henry Francis du Pont Winterthur Museum, Route 52, Winterthur, Delaware 19735.
Historic Deerfield, The Street, Deerfield, Massachusetts 01342.
Museum of Fine Arts, 465 Huntington Avenue, Boston, Massachusetts 02115.